How to behave in church

How to behave in church

PETER JEFFERY

 EVANGELICAL PRESS

EVANGELICAL PRESS
12 Wooler Street, Darlington, Co. Durham, DL1 1RQ,
England

© Evangelical Press 1994
First published 1994

**British Library Cataloguing in Publication Data
available**

ISBN 0 85234 318 3

Scripture quotations in this publication are from the Holy
Bible, New International Version. Copyright © 1973, 1978,
1984, International Bible Society. Published by Hodder &
Stoughton.

Printed and bound in Great Britain at Cox & Wyman,
Reading

'I am writing you these instructions so that, if I am delayed, you will know how people ought to conduct themselves in God's household, which is the church of the living God, the pillar and foundation of the truth' (1 Timothy 3:14-15).

Contents

Introduction:
A note on Timothy

Timothy, the man to whom the epistle which forms the basis of our study was addressed, was converted as a young man during Paul's first visit to Lystra. His father was a Greek and his mother a Jewess. When Paul visited Lystra again (Acts 16:1-3), Timothy joined him in his ministry. This took place around A.D. 50. For about sixteen years Timothy worked with Paul in the spread of the gospel and the care of the churches. He not only accompanied the apostle but was also entrusted with ministry on his own (1 Thess. 3:1; 1 Cor. 4:17). Paul clearly had a very high regard for Timothy, particularly because of his pastoral heart. He tells the Phillippians, 'I have no one else like him, who takes a genuine interest in your welfare.' So when the church at Ephesus needed a pastor, it was Timothy that Paul sent there. He had many commendable qualities, but he also had certain weaknesses that made the work at Ephesus difficult for him.

He was young, possibly in his mid-thirties, and this could be a serious hindrance in dealing with older and awkward Christians. Paul has to warn him, 'Don't let anyone look down on you because you are young' (1 Tim. 4:12). Physically he was not very strong, and he was prone to frequent illnesses (1 Tim. 5:23). His temperament made him naturally shy and fearful. Paul urges the Corinthians to bear this in mind when Timothy visits them, and he asks them to help the younger man settle among them (1 Cor. 16:10-11). 'This, then,' to quote John Stott, 'was Timothy — young in years, frail in physique, retiring in disposition — who nevertheless was called to exacting responsibilities in the church of God. Greatness was being thrust upon him, and like Moses and Jeremiah and a host of others before and after him, Timothy was exceedingly reluctant to accept it.'

Paul knew all this and was concerned for his young friend. The apostle had just been released from his first imprisonment in Rome and in about A.D. 66-67 he wrote to Timothy to encourage him and to advise him on how to cope as the leader of a Christian church.

1.
The nature and role of the church

We are living in days of free expression with a corresponding resentment of authority, order and discipline. Sadly this has penetrated the church and she faces a crisis of authority. This is not something new. Twice in the book of Judges (17:6; 21:25) we read, 'In those days Israel had no king; everyone did as he saw fit.' No king meant no authority, and no authority meant anarchy. But the church has a King: he is 'the King eternal, immortal, invisible, the only God' (1 Tim. 1:17); therefore the authority of that King must be preeminent in the church. Men cannot do merely what they deem to be fit. There is a way in which we are to conduct ourselves in church.

Paul's first epistle to Timothy was written to tell us that way. Here we see the King, or Head of the church, the leaders of the church, the members and the problems.

There is also a great deal said on the role of women in the church, and on the vexed question of the church and money. All these issues are dealt with so that we may know 'how people ought to conduct themselves in God's household, which is the church of the living God' (1 Tim. 3:15).

It is obvious from these words that there is a right way and a wrong way to behave in church. It is also clear that the right way does not come naturally to a man, even when the man is a Christian. Timothy was a Christian — he was a pastor — but the implication of 1 Timothy 3:15 is that if Paul had not written to tell him, even he would not have known how people ought to conduct themselves. And Paul only knew because he was writing under the inspiration of the Holy Spirit. Church life is not dictated by the current whim of society or by the fancies and desires of its members.

What is the church?

The church is not a man-made institution; it is God's household. He is the Head and he sets the standards. God does this with love and care, and these standards cover various things from our attitudes — no anger or disputing (1 Tim. 2:8) — to our dress (1 Tim. 2:9).

When Paul refers to the church he is not talking about a building. The church is not a building of stone or brick or any other material. More often than not the members of a church may gather in a particular building which we may call a church, but that is not important. The church is the people of God, those who belong to God and gather together to worship him. The building in which a church meets could be destroyed by fire but the church itself would still be intact, because the church consists of men and women saved by the grace of God who, living in fellowship with God the Father, God the Son and God the Holy Spirit, gather together for worship, praise, instruction and fellowship.

The church, wrote A. W. Tozer, 'is the temple in which the Spirit of Christ dwells, the body of which Christ is the Head, the medium through which he works for the reclamation of mankind. Individual members of the church working in harmony with each other are the lips and hands and feet of the inliving Christ. The Church is the true Shekinah, the visible habitation of the invisible God, the Bride of Christ, destined to share for ever the love of his heart and the privileges of his throne.'

It is a company of people who by nature are sinners but have been saved by the grace of God: 'Here is a trustworthy saying that deserves full acceptance: Christ

Jesus came into the world to save sinners — of whom I am the worst' (1 Tim. 1:15).

The church, then, is people, God's people, and what we are being told in 1 Timothy is how to conduct ourselves when we come together as Christians. We are a redeemed people, but we are not a perfect people and, therefore, there are often many problems in the church. Most of Paul's letters in the New Testament were written to deal with church problems. Problems in a church are not exceptional — the devil will see to that, but no Christian has the right to absent himself from church attendance because he wants to avoid hassle. Some Christians are far too sensitive about their own feelings and position, and they need the hurly-burly of church life to humble them and remind them that they are not the only Christians with feelings. Hassle can be good for our sanctification as it throws us more and more upon the Lord for grace, patience and understanding. This does not justify tension between believers, but learning how to deal with tensions in a Christ-honouring way can promote a real growth in grace. Christians need the church for its problems as well as its blessings.

New Testament practice

The New Testament uses the word 'church' in two ways. First, there is the use as in Ephesians 5:25: 'Christ loved the church and gave himself up for her.' Here the reference is to the universal church, the whole company of the redeemed in every place, at every time. It is *the* church, the church to which all Christians belong the moment they are saved.

Then there is the use as in 1 Corinthians 1:2: 'To the church of God in Corinth'. Here the reference is to the local church, the Christians in the city of Corinth who met for worship and fellowship in a particular place. It is not *the* church, but *a* local church.

Throughout the New Testament it is assumed that every believer attends a local church. It is taken for granted that Christians, who from the moment they are saved become members of the universal church, should associate themselves with fellow believers in their town or city. Christians need each other. From the example of Jesus, who on the Sabbath day went into the synagogue 'as was his custom' (Luke 4:16), to the behaviour of the new converts after Pentecost, who continued to meet together (Acts 2:46), right up to the command of Hebrews 10:25, 'Let us not give up meeting together', the New Testament encourages and exhorts the value and importance of going to church.

Teaching

It is God's intention that we grow in the Christian faith, and one of the main functions of the church is to help this growth. To this end we are told in Ephesians 4:11 that God gives to certain men in the church the ability to teach and expound the meaning of Scripture. Their function is 'to prepare God's people for works of service, so that the body of Christ may be built up until we all reach unity in the faith and in the knowledge of the Son of God and become mature, attaining to the whole measure of the fulness of Christ' (Eph. 4:12-13). If we go on to read Ephesians 4:14-16, we shall see that it is God's intention that spiritual infants should grow up into mature believers. The teaching and preaching of the church are God-given instruments in achieving this. Benefiting from the preaching is so important that we shall devote the whole of the next chapter to this subject.

Some Christians think they do not need to go to church for teaching. They say, 'We have the Bible and the Holy Spirit to guide us, so we need nothing else.' To put it at its mildest, this is arrogant nonsense. It is to put oneself above the teaching which God in his wisdom has deemed necessary for the church.

Discipline

The leaders of a local church will realize that one of their God-given responsibilities is to administer discipline in the church. It is a great privilege for a Christian, as part of the local church, to be under pastoral discipline. To have older, mature Christians who care enough about your spiritual growth to rebuke you when you are wrong is nothing but a privilege.

Today discipline has become almost a dirty word in many sections of society. Everyone wants to do just as he or she pleases. That is the attitude of the world. The Christian can live no longer by that attitude because what he or she does or says affects other Christians and, more importantly, brings either glory or shame on God's name. If you do wrong, it is necessary for your own well-being (Gal. 6:1), for the peace of the church (Rom. 16:17) and for the honour of God that you be told.

Will you be willing to accept this discipline if and

when it is necessary? It would do us all good to heed the advice of Tozer: 'Keep your heart open to the correction of the Lord and be ready to receive his chastisement regardless of who holds the whip. The great saints all learnt to take a licking gracefully — and that may be one reason why they were great saints.'

Fellowship

When God saved you he did not mean you to live in isolation. You are meant to be part of the church and to enjoy fellowship with other believers. One of the most beautiful things you discover after conversion is the blessed bond you have with other Christians. God's people are drawn from all types of background, rich and poor, black and white, clever and dull; yet they are all one in Christ. All barriers fall before the redeeming love of Jesus (Eph. 2:14-16; Gal. 3:26-28). The New Testament abounds with examples of this. Among the twelve apostles were Simon the Zealot, the ardent Jewish nationalist, and also Matthew the tax collector, the servant of the hated Romans. These two men would normally have despised each other, but in Christ they were one.

18

Fellowship is not a matter of a few Christians talking together about the weather, their holidays, or engaging in social chit-chat. This, of course, can be quite enjoyable and there is no harm in Christians having fun together. But the uniqueness of Christian fellowship consists in being able to talk about and share together the joys, blessings and problems of our faith.

Fellowship is like the spokes of a wheel. The closer the spokes are to the hub, the closer they are to each other. The further away they are from the hub, the further they are from each other. In the same way, the closer you are to the Lord, the closer you will be to other believers. The more you enjoy fellowship with Christ, the more you will enjoy the fellowship of his people.

The officers and members of the church

We also learn from 1 Timothy that the church has order and structure. It has pastors, elders and deacons. But it is God's church. He, the living God, is its Head.

We must appreciate how important this is in re-lationship to the verses in Judges quoted at the begin-ning of this chapter. If someone does not recognize God as the Lord and Jesus as the King, he will think he

19

can do what he sees fit in church. So if the church is to behave in a way pleasing to its King it must consist only of those who love the King and submit to his authority. In other words, it must consist only of Christians, and Christians as defined in 1 Timothy 1:12-16 — sinners saved by grace. Anyone can come into the building — indeed everyone is most welcome — but the church must consist only of saved sinners who are living under the authority of King Jesus. For this reason a church membership roll is important. If there is no membership then all who attend services in that particular building, Christians and non-Christians, could, and often do, assume they are members. So non-Christians would assume they have the right, because of their attendance, to have a say in the running of the church.

Sadly this has all too often happened and the lordship of Christ is eroded. A membership list is not a foolproof way of maintaining the purity of the church, but it does go a long way towards this end if the membership is restricted to born-again Christians. All believers should see to it that they are members of their church, not merely to have their name on a list, but to help maintain the kingship of Christ in that place.

The purity of the church

By purity I mean the church conducting itself in a way that pleases its King, and this can only be possible when its members are Christians living in submission to the authority of the Word of God. This purity is particularly important in the light of the statement in 1 Timothy 3:15 that the church is the pillar and foundation of the truth.

This is an amazing statement. As in some great building where the pillars support the roof and the foundations support the whole superstructure, so the church supports the truth of God. If the church is weak and moves its position, the truth will come crashing down. It is true that Christ is the foundation of the church, but we are reminded here that God in his wisdom has laid upon the church the awesome responsibility of proclaiming and defending his truth in a world that is hostile to it. This responsibility is given not to the pastors, elders and deacons, but to the whole church. For this reason it is vitally important that we know how to conduct ourselves in the church, because if our conduct is wrong and the foundation and pillars begin to move, the truth is in danger.

21

Paul is very concerned with this and in 1 Timothy 1:19-20 he gives an example of how serious it is: 'Some have rejected these and so have shipwrecked their faith. Among them are Hymenaeus and Alexander, whom I have handed over to Satan to be taught not to blaspheme.' Wrong doctrine is not to be tolerated in the church and it must be dealt with swiftly and decisively. We shall see what this means in a later chapter. Throughout this short epistle Paul is primarily concerned with maintaining the truth in the church. Most things are seen in the light of this. For example, his teaching on the role of women in the church (1 Tim. 2:11-15) is based on the fact that it was Eve who was deceived first and turned from the truth. In 1 Timothy 5 when he is dealing with the social responsibilities of the church, a failure to meet our obligations is seen as a denial of the truth of the faith. Even the Christian in his daily work is to conduct himself in such a way 'that God's name and our teaching may not be slandered' (1 Tim. 6:1).

The church supports and upholds the truth not only by its doctrine but also by its life, and this means the life of all its members. So yet again we see how important it is that we conduct ourselves in church in a God-honouring manner.

2.
How to listen to preaching

Good preaching will not be profitable to you unless it is accompanied by good listening. In turn, good listening will encourage good preaching. Christians need to give more thought to how they listen to God's Word when it is preached.

The importance of preaching to the individual Christian and to the life of the church is emphasized in the following quotations: 'I warn everyone who loves his soul to be jealous as to the preaching he regularly hears and the place of worship he regularly attends. He who deliberately settles down under a ministry which is unsound is a very unwise man. If false doctrine is preached in a church a man who loves his soul is not right in going to that church' (J. C. Ryle). 'The most urgent need in the Christian church today is true preaching; and as it is the greatest and most urgent need in the church, it is obviously the greatest need of the world also' (D. M. Lloyd-Jones).

If this is true then we need to value preaching as a God-given vehicle by which we are meant to profit from Scripture, and this will produce in us a right attitude when we hear preaching. To appreciate this, let us turn to Nehemiah 8 and read the first twelve verses. From this passage we learn what true preaching is and how to listen to it.

The background

The Old Testament is full of dramatic scenes: scenes full of people and incident; scenes of historical importance like the Exodus, and Elijah on Carmel. Nehemiah 8 comes into this category. There were 50,000 people gathered around a wooden pulpit in the open air by the Water Gate in Jerusalem. It was a city with strong walls that had just been rebuilt, but with houses still in ruins (7:4).

Why were the people there? Why did they make the wooden platform or pulpit? The event took place in about 445 B.C., but the events that really led up to it started many years prior to this date when Nebuchadnezzar and his Babylonian army attacked and destroyed Jerusalem and took many of the population into exile and slavery. The Scriptures make it clear that this was not merely another political instance of a stronger nation conquering a weaker one. This was God's judgement upon his people because of their idolatry, unbelief and disobedience. So for many years the Hebrew people were in exile under God's judgement. God did not totally reject them, because they were his people and he loved them, so even in exile he sent them prophets like Jeremiah and Ezekiel.

The exile eventually ended and some returned to Jerusalem, firstly under Ezra and then Nehemiah. After building the temple they started to rebuild the city, with special emphasis upon rebuilding the walls for security. Under Nehemiah's inspired leadership the walls were rebuilt in fifty-two days of hard and dangerous work. Having done that, they built the pulpit and gathered to hear God's Word.

Do you see what happened? Why did they build the pulpit? Because they had finished building the walls and wanted to thank God and hear his Word. But why did they have to rebuild the walls in the first place? Because for many years they had been in exile in Babylon and the walls had decayed through neglect. God had now brought them back to the place they should never have left many years previously, namely the pulpit and his Word. If they had been as eager then as they were now to hear and obey the Word of God, they would never have had to suffer the Babylonian exile.

Here is a basic lesson repeated time and time again in the history of God's people. When we turn away from the Word of God and reject its authority and teaching, then inevitably judgement follows. There will come a time when God allows the enemy to invade and there is a spiritual exile, humiliation and weakness. At the end of the twentieth century we are living in such a period. At the beginning of this century there was a rejection of the truth of the Word by liberal theology. This led to a rejection of the preaching of the Word, and the Christian church can never go down this dark path without reaping the consequences we see all around us today.

There are several ways of rejecting preaching. Liberal theology's mistrust of Scripture reduced preaching to a ten-minute exercise in morality or politics. Evangelical Christians did not make this mistake but we too can lose faith in the effectiveness of preaching and fill our services with music and drama, so that the preaching becomes nothing more than an appendix at the end. Another danger for evangelicals is that expressed in Ezekiel 33:30-32: 'As for you, son of man, your countrymen are talking together about you by the walls and at the doors of the houses, saying to each other, "Come and hear the message that has come from the Lord." My people come to you, as they usually do, and sit before you to listen to your words, but they do not put them into practice. With their mouths they express devotion, but their hearts are greedy for unjust gain. Indeed, to them you are nothing more than one who sings love songs with a beautiful voice and plays an instrument well, for they hear your words but do not put them into practice.' It is possible to enjoy preaching as a type of entertainment but with no intention of taking it seriously.

God's way

In times of spiritual weakness God has rescued his church time after time by the preaching of Scripture. The church was born on a recognition of the truth of the Word as the apostles, enlightened by the Holy Spirit, saw the truth and preached it. The Acts of the Apostles is full of preaching and this is what 'turned the world upside down'. In the fourth century, when the church turned from the Word to the tradition of men, a great spiritual deadness set in that lasted for over a thousand

27

years. Then in the sixteenth century God came to the rescue with the Reformation. This move of the Holy Spirit inspired a tremendous turning back to the Word of God and to a preaching of it. In the eighteenth century the church in Britain was Protestant but spiritually dead — then God raised up preachers. Men like George Whitefield, John and Charles Wesley, Daniel Rowland, Howel Harris and Jonathan Edwards preached with power and turned their nations back to God.

This is not just true historically; it is also a biblical principle. Romans 10 starts with Paul's great desire and prayer that the Israelites should be saved. But they cannot be saved unless they hear the Word (vv. 14-15), and they will not hear unless someone preaches to them. And even then not any preacher will do, but only one sent by God.

In the light of all this, we have to seriously ask ourselves, do we have a love and respect for God's chosen way of making known the gospel? Do we love to hear God's Word expounded?

The preacher

It is very interesting to note in Nehemiah 8 that the preacher was Ezra and not Nehemiah. Nehemiah was

God's instrument to get the walls built. Ezra had been in Jerusalem for several years before Nehemiah arrived and little progress had been made in repairing the walls. Under Nehemiah's leadership and drive the work was done in fifty-two days. He was a powerhouse, the organizer, the inspiration on the human level for this vital work; but now the walls were up and the Word was to be preached, and Nehemiah was not a preacher, but Ezra was. Nehemiah was a godly man, blessed and used by God, but he was not a preacher.

The principle that Paul sets before us in Romans 10 is one that God always adheres to and therefore one that the church must always take seriously: 'How can they preach unless they are sent?' It is God who decides who preaches. He calls men to this ministry and equips them for the task. This is why preaching is such a solemn responsibility. The church has to recognize this and be careful whom it allows into the pulpit. The fact that a man is born again and a faithful follower of Christ does not in itself qualify him to preach.

Christians ought not to listen to the preaching of men who are not called by God. And Christians should certainly not help to financially support men who deny the truth. A Christian lady once phoned the pastor of another church to tell him that she had been witnessing to a teenage girl and this girl was now willing to go to church. She asked if the pastor could arrange for some girls from his church to meet the teenager and take her to hear him preach. He said he would do that, but then asked this lady why she did not take her young friend to her own church. She replied, 'I cannot do that because she will never hear the gospel in my church.' She was then asked what she, a Christian, was doing in a church where the gospel was not preached. I am thankful to say, she took the point, left the non-gospel-preaching church and became a faithful and useful member in a true church.

Ezra stood up in the pulpit that day in Jerusalem because God had called him to this special ministry of preaching. You can see something of the evidence of this call in Ezra 7:10: 'For Ezra had devoted himself to the study and observance of the Law of the Lord and to teaching its decrees and laws in Israel.' There are three things here: firstly, Ezra learned the Word; secondly, he lived it; and only then, thirdly, did he preach it.

The support

When Ezra stood up to preach he was not alone. We read in verses 4 and 7 of a number of men who stood with him. This is similar to the first-ever Christian sermon in Acts 2, where we read in verse 14 that 'Peter stood up with the eleven.' The preacher should never stand alone. He will always need the support of the people of God. That support will take several forms but pre-eminently it will mean prayer support. You will never get much out of the preaching of a man you only criticize and never pray for. Paul's frequent requests for prayer support show the urgency of this. Charles Spurgeon was once asked what was the secret of his remarkable ministry. He answered simply, 'My people pray for me.'

What should Christians pray for the preacher? Above all things, pray for unction — that inexplicable power of God upon the proclaiming of the Word. Samuel Davies, the American preacher and hymn-writer, commented the first time he heard George Whitefield preach: 'The sermon was ordinary but the unction was extraordinary.'

Your prayer will be of immense value to the preacher but it will also be of value to you as you listen. Prayer for preaching encourages expectancy and an eagerness to listen. Christians often say, 'I got nothing out of that sermon.' Perhaps it would be more profitable if they asked, 'What did I put into it?' The more prayer you put into your pastor's sermons, the more likely you are to be blessed by them.

The content

Ezra opened the book and preached the book. The result was that the people 'understood the words that had been made known to them' (Neh. 8:12). There are two important things about preaching — the *how* and the *what*. How a man preaches — clearly, interestingly, with illustration and application — is of great importance, but so too is what he preaches. The content of the sermon is of prime importance and verse 8 is an excellent example for all preachers: 'They read from the Book of the Law of God, making it clear and giving the meaning so that the people could understand what was being read.' The purpose of preaching is to expound the Scriptures and make God known to the people. Exposition is the best way to ensure that all the truths of God are preached and it is the most satisfying of all preaching for the hungry soul to listen to.

There are many preachers with a fund of funny stories and witty illustrations that can entertain a congregation, but do they feed the souls of men and women? The great joy of verse 12 was produced by an understanding of Scripture.

The congregation

In verses 2 and 3 the congregation is described as being made up of men and women and all who were able to understand. The phrase 'able to understand' must refer to children who had reached an age, perhaps eight or nine or ten years old, when they could benefit from the sermon. Evangelical churches today could learn a great deal from this. In many churches children of believers go out in the morning service just before the sermon and are never brought to an evening service. Consequently they never hear the Word of God preached. As a parent myself I know the dangers of forcing children to go to church, but there is a greater danger of depriving them of the blessing of hearing God's Word preached. If they are capable of understanding they ought to be with their parents listening to the sermon.

In verses 3 to 6 we are shown the attitude of this congregation as they listened. Firstly, they were attentive. This was God's Word and they were afraid to miss a single word. There was no need for funny stories to capture their attention. These people were eager to hear before the preacher got into the pulpit.

Next we see the respect they had for God's Word. When Ezra opened the book they all stood up. This was

33

not an organized or ceremonial act, but the spon-
taneous response of people who loved the Scriptures.
I am not suggesting that we turn this action into a
ceremony, but there is no doubt that when there is a
respect like this for the Word then faithful preaching
will always be a source of blessing. We have seen that
Christians often say at the end of a service, 'I didn't get
much out of that sermon.' Maybe there were faults in
the preaching, but what about the listening? Was there
an eager expectancy? Was there a listening spirit? An
ordinary preacher can be turned into a good preacher
by a congregation like the one to which Ezra preached.

Not only did this congregation listen well, but they
also responded with feeling and passion to what they
heard. They lifted up their hands and responded, 'Amen!
Amen!' For some Christians this is a problem. They see
other believers who abuse this response and turn it into
a meaningless gesture. So they themselves reject it
altogether. We say, 'We do not lift up our arms or say
"Amen" in our church.' Maybe not, but they did in
Jerusalem when Ezra preached, and they did in the
New Testament churches. It seems from 1 Corinthians
14:16 that the 'Amen' was a usual part of Christian
worship. Charles Hodge tells us that 'Amen is a Hebrew adjective signifying "true" or "faithful", and this

34

was common in synagogue worship.' Hodge goes on to quote Justin Martyr, a Christian leader of the second century, who said that the custom passed over to the Christian church. The same can be said of the lifting up of the hands in 1 Timothy 2:8. As far as Paul was concerned this was normal in worship. It is true that in the passage in 1 Timothy the important thing is not the position of the hands, but the spiritual disposition of the man offering the prayer; none the less the lifting up of hands is acknowledged as an acceptable part of New Testament worship.

As Ezra's congregation listened to the Word being expounded, they worshipped the Lord. There is no greater stimulant to worship than preaching in the power of the Spirit. As the Word is preached, our hearts and minds respond to the biblical truths and instinctively we are praising and thanking God. We may be convicted or humbled, encouraged or thrilled, but we are worshipping our God and Saviour. To think of worship as merely singing hymns is to miss the whole point of preaching. We cannot truly worship without an awareness of God. The truths expressed in good hymns can give us this, but how much more the inspired truths of Scripture faithfully preached!

The response of the congregation was first weeping

with conviction of sin (Neh. 8:9), and then joy (Neh. 8:12) at the mercy and grace of God. Such a response is the product of good preaching and good listening. May the Lord grant us more of both!

3.
The God of the church

The Christian church is a great church because its Head, its God, is a great God. The head of the church is not the queen, nor the pope or some archbishop, but the true and living God. In 1 Timothy Paul brings before us great truths concerning who God is in three magnificent doxologies. A doxology is a liturgical formula of praise to God. It is interesting to note where Paul places these doxologies in this letter.

The first is in 1 Timothy 1:17: 'Now to the King eternal, immortal, invisible, the only God, be honour and glory for ever and ever. Amen.' This comes at the end of a consideration of the grace of God in salvation.

The second is in 1 Timothy 3:16: 'Beyond all question, the mystery of godliness is great: he appeared in a body, was vindicated by the Spirit, was seen by angels, was preached among the nations, was believed on in the world, was taken up in glory', and follows Paul's thoughts of God's goodness to us in and through the church.

The third doxology comes immediately after the second coming of the Lord Jesus Christ is mentioned: 'God, the blessed and only Ruler, the King of kings and Lord of lords, who alone is immortal and who lives in unapproachable light, whom no one has seen or can see. To him be honour and might for ever. Amen' (1 Tim. 6:15-16).

In other words, as the great apostle considers and meditates on the activity of God, particularly God in the person of the Lord Jesus Christ, he finds himself bursting into songs of praise in adoration of the full majesty and glory of his God. This pattern of Paul's is a good example to us in our worship of almighty God. First he thinks of what God has done; then his heart responds to his thinking and he feels the wonder and glory of these truths. This inevitably erupts in praise and adoration for the character and being of God. True worship will always start with thinking and then proceed to feeling. Charles Wesley longed for 'a heart to praise [his] God'. What sort of heart will this be? It will be a heart that always feels 'the blood, so freely shed for me'. The answer for a Christian who complains of a cold heart and who does not feel like worshipping is for him to start thinking about what God has done for him. The biblical answer to a cold heart is a thinking mind. To quote Wesley's hymn again, the heart that feels is also 'a heart in every thought renewed and full of love divine'. It is as we contemplate and meditate on who God is and what he has done, that our hearts are warmed and motivated to worship and praise.

In Paul's first epistle to Timothy we are told many things about God.

The only God (1 Tim. 1:17)

This truth makes Christians intolerant of other so-called gods. 'We know that an idol is nothing' (1 Cor. 8:4-5). As Paul says, there are many gods, which are the creation of the minds and hands of men, but the psalmist spells out for us in very clear terms the value of these so-called gods:

'They have mouths, but cannot speak,
    eyes, but they cannot see;
they have ears, but cannot hear,
    noses, but they cannot smell;

they have hands, but cannot feel,
    feet but they cannot walk;
nor can they utter a sound with their throats'
                                (Ps. 115:5-7).

Our God is the only God because he is the only living God. He sees, he hears, he knows, he speaks. Because of this we can have a real and meaningful relationship with him. Such a God loves and acts, and in turn promotes love in us for himself.

It is often objected that Christians should not be intolerant of other religions because all paths lead to God. No, says the Bible, that is not true. 'For there is one God and one mediator between God and men, the man Christ Jesus' (1 Tim. 2:5). Our God is the only God and Jesus is the only Saviour, and therefore the only way to God.

The eternal God (1 Tim. 1:17)

The truth of the eternity of God opens up to us many precious and encouraging thoughts. It means that what he was, he still is. What he did, he can still do if he so chooses. When we realize this all the stories and actions of God in the Bible come into the realm of possible Christian experience. If he so chooses, the eternal God can repeat each and every action of the past. It is true that there are some actions, like the death of his Son, that he will never repeat because there is no need for it, but there is nothing beyond his eternal power.

The eternal God means that he is always there to help and minister to his people. 'The Lord is the everlasting God' (Isa. 40:28). 'But from everlasting to everlasting the Lord's love is with those who fear him' (Ps. 103:17). We are so used to change and decay and death, but the eternal God stands above all such things. He says, 'I the Lord do not change' (Mal. 3:6).

The unconquerable God (1 Tim. 6:15)

'The only Ruler, the King of kings, the Lord of lords' puts our God into a category all of his own. Who can possibly hope to challenge and overcome such a God? The history of the world is full of men and systems who raised their fists in anger against God and challenged his authority. Their defeat is obvious to all. Even the devil, that mighty evil one, and all his satanic hosts fall when they seek to challenge the King of kings and Lord of lords.

41

What a tremendous confidence and hope this produces in the heart of every Christian who can say, 'This is my God!'

The immortal God (1 Tim. 1:17; 6:16)

God alone is immortal. This means that God alone has life in and of himself. He is the source and fountain of life. The life of every created being finds its source in God. Every Christian, every atheist, lives and moves and owes his existence to God, but God owes his existence to no one. He is immortal.

Immortality means more than endless existence. It really speaks of the fulness and blessedness of life that is in God. The souls of all men made in the image of God are immortal in the sense that they have an endless existence. But for the Christian immortality is something different. It is the product of the gospel. According to 2 Timothy 1:10, life and immortality are brought to light through the gospel. As William Hendriksen puts it, 'For the believer immortality is therefore a redemptive concept. It is everlasting salvation. For God it is eternal blessedness. But while the believer has received immortality, as one receives a drink of water from a fountain, God has it. It belongs to his very being. He is himself the fountain.'

42

The invisible God (1 Tim. 1:17; 6:16)

This means that God is beyond human examination. He cannot be put under a microscope and examined or probed. If God is to be known it will only be to those to whom he chooses to reveal himself.

There is an awesomeness about God that baffles all human understanding and reason. He is totally unlike anything we can know or experience. Yet amazingly we can see the invisible. Moses saw God by faith (Heb. 11:27). Faith allows us to see through the dazzling light that surrounds God and appreciate something of the wonder of God. Even more amazingly, we can love the invisible: 'Though you have not seen him, you love him; and even though you do not see him now, you believe in him and are filled with an inexpressible and glorious joy' (1 Peter 1:8).

The incarnate God (1 Tim. 3:16)

God is immortal and invisible, yet he appeared in a body. God became man. Here is probably the most staggering truth about God: 'our God contracted to a span, incomprehensibly made man', to quote Charles

43

Wesley again. Jesus Christ is God incarnate, God in the flesh. Jesus is, says Paul in Colossians 1:15, 'the image of the invisible God'.

Without God becoming incarnate there could never have been one single Christian, and consequently there could never have been a church. But there is a church and how privileged that church is that its God loved it so much as to leave heaven, become man, bear the sin of man, die in man's place and purchase for the church the salvation that distinguishes its members from all other men and women! Jesus is the Head and King of the church because it belongs to him. He has purchased it with his own blood.

It is because of all these great truths about God that Christians need to think deeply on how they conduct themselves in church. The church is God's church; therefore what God requires must be the only consideration. What is the will of Jesus must be the watchword. And we can ask this in the sure knowledge that Jesus has a will and purpose for his church. The right and only conduct for the Christian, therefore, is to seek, know and do the will of him who is King of kings, Lord of lords, the immortal and invisible God.

4.
The members of the church

The church consists of sinners who have been saved by the grace of God. If someone refuses to acknowledge he is a sinner then he has no place in the membership of the church. He is welcome to attend the services but should never be given the impression that he is a member of the church of Jesus Christ. If a person does acknowledge that he is a sinner but believes he can take care of the problem himself, then he too has no place in the membership of the church. The church of Jesus Christ consists only of sinners who have repented of their sin and come in faith to Christ for forgiveness. They know they cannot save themselves and put their hope solely in the grace and mercy of God. Paul was the founder of the church at Ephesus but he said to Timothy in 1 Timothy 1:13: 'I was once a blasphemer and a persecutor and a violent man.' With regard to the world in general Paul was morally, socially and religiously of impeccable reputation, but with regard to Christ and the church he was a blasphemer, a persecutor and a violent man. He had an obsession against Christians and because of his hatred of them his persecution knew no bounds (Acts 26:11). How did such a man ever become a Christian? He tells us in 1 Timothy 1:14-15: 'The grace of our Lord was poured out on me abundantly, along with the faith and love that are in Christ Jesus. Here is a trustworthy saying that deserves full acceptance: Christ Jesus came into the world to save sinners — of whom I am the worst.'

Paul did not change himself. God did something for him and to him, and God does the same for all who become Christians. Timothy was never a blasphemer or persecutor. On the contrary, we are told about him that 'From infancy you have known the holy Scriptures, which are able to make you wise for salvation through faith in Christ Jesus' (2 Tim. 3:15). But for both Timothy and Paul, and for each of us, God has come into our lives with saving grace or we would for ever remain sinners under the divine wrath. God sent Christ Jesus into the world to save sinners. What sort of sinners does Jesus save? All sorts: men like Paul — the worst kind of sinner; men like Timothy — nice, gentle, brought up in a Christian home, but still a sinner. In

1 Timothy 2:6 Paul tells Timothy how Jesus saves sinners: '... who gave himself as a ransom for all men.'

Sin enslaves. It wraps men up in ignorance and unbelief (1 Tim. 1:13), and there is no greater slavery than this. It blinds men to the beauty of Jesus and the holiness of God. It is so absolute a bondage that men do not even know they are in it. Jesus came to ransom these captives, to pay the price to set them free. This he did when he died upon the cross because we are redeemed by his blood, that is, by his atoning death. As a consequence of this, grace, faith and love (1 Tim. 1:14) are poured out abundantly upon us.

That is how Paul and Timothy became Christians. If God did this for Paul, the worst of sinners, then, the apostle argues in 1 Timothy 1:16, he will do it for all who believe on him. God 'wants all men to be saved' (1 Tim. 2:4), so there is hope for us all.

Church members are not perfect

The only way to be a member of the church is to be a Christian, and the only way to be a Christian is through confession of our sin to God and faith in the Lord Jesus Christ as the only Saviour. The church consists of sinners saved by grace, but they are still sinners and not perfect. They are completely justified, but not completely sanctified. This is a most important factor to remember as we address ourselves to the purpose of this epistle and how people ought to conduct themselves in God's church.

The church is made up of men and women, not unfallen angels; therefore the conduct of its members will not always be what it ought to be. This is not to excuse bad behaviour, but it does explain it. In this world there will never be a perfect church. As we saw in chapter 1, many of the New Testament epistles were written to deal with problems in the local church. We must recognize this and make sure that we are not the problem in our own church. One major source of problems is that we set too low a standard for ourselves and too high a standard for other believers. We expect more from them than we are prepared to give ourselves. For instance, if we are ill and no one from the church visits us we are upset, but do we visit others when they are ill?

None of us is perfect in our attitudes, behaviour or understanding, so let us all exercise a little tolerance. This does not mean that we should excuse sin — the New Testament will not allow us to do that — but it will help us to be more caring and loving. Probably the most difficult church in the New Testament era was Corinth.

48

This church was riddled with problems and as Paul was trying to deal with some of the most contentious issues in 1 Corinthians 12 and 14, he sandwiches between these two chapters the amazing passage on love: 'Love is patient, love is kind. It does not envy, it does not boast, it is not proud. It is not rude, it is not self-seeking, it is not easily angered, it keeps no record of wrongs. Love does not delight in evil but rejoices with the truth. It always protects, always trusts, always hopes, always perseveres' (1 Cor. 13:4-7).

We all have our weaknesses

Because we are sinners the exercise of the love described in 1 Corinthians 13 is vital for the well-being of the church. Never forget that the church has a great enemy, Satan, who will play on our weaknesses to upset the church. As sinners we all have our own particular weaknesses and we must learn to recognize them. If we do not, the devil will use them to wreck the church. It is probably true that more churches are split over petty personality squabbles among believers than over false doctrine.

What is your particular weakness? Are you impatient, critical, envious, unforgiving, angry, resentful, intolerant, self-opinionated? You can be a born-again Christian and have any or all of these sins. The devil is delighted because you can then be of more use to him in wrecking a church than any heretic. Every Christian needs to be honest with him or herself and recognize a particular weakness and deal with it.

If you tend to be critical, then keep your mouth closed. If you are self-opinionated, let others speak and try, try, try to understand their viewpoint. If you are envious, do not feed this weakness and do not let others feed it. If you are quick to take offence, remember it is possible to *give* offence unintentionally but it is not possible to *take* offence unintentionally. Instead of calling this weakness a sensitive spirit, call it what it is — admit that you are touchy. You will be more likely to deal with it then.

The church consists of sinners, and thank God for that, but beware lest your sin disrupts your church.

5.
The leaders of the church

Paul's first epistle to Timothy has much to say on the leadership of the church. For instance, in chapter 3 we have overseers (bishop and elder is the same office as overseer) and deacons. Here are two distinct types of leaders and we are instructed on the qualities men need to occupy these positions. But what of Timothy? Was he an elder or a deacon? It is clear from the epistle that Timothy's function was pastoral, caring for the spiritual well-being of the Christians. Connected with this was a ministry of preaching and teaching (see 1 Tim. 1:3; 4:6,11,13; 6:17,20). The pastoral ministry is part of the function of eldership, as we shall see in this chapter.

In the New Testament no such office as pope or archbishop or priest is recognized in the church. The leadership is in the hands of elders and deacons. It is important that we see this as the biblical pattern and not merely a matter of church tradition, because this will affect how we conduct ourselves in church.

Structure

It is God's will that his church should have structure and this includes the leadership of elders and deacons. This is because men and women need leadership. Without it things would not be done decently and in order because, as sinners, we are more prone to chaos than order. Examples of this abound in the New Testament.

There is the chaos of wrong doctrine (1 Tim. 1:3-7). Who is to deal with this? Paul tells Timothy that it is his responsibility as the pastor/elder of the church. It is a spiritual problem and those men called elders are charged to deal with it (1 Tim. 3:4-5).

There is the chaos of bad management which we see in Acts 6. Who is to deal with this? The apostles could have dealt with this problem themselves, but that would have meant neglecting their prime ministry of prayer and preaching. So men that we normally recognize as deacons were chosen to deal with it and they did so with sensitivity and skill.

All chaos, whether spiritual or material, will hinder the progress of the gospel, so God decrees that men with certain spiritual qualities and gifts be appointed so that such problems may be avoided, or if not avoided, then dealt with swiftly when they arise.

Difficulties of leadership

No leader of God's people has ever had an easy task. Consider for a moment two of the greatest leaders in Scripture. Moses and Paul had to endure an almost continual barrage of criticism from God's people. Why was this? It was because of the nature of spiritual leadership. Human nature polluted by sin likes to please itself and resents being told it *must* do something. Sadly, this is also true of the Christian, and the devil will inflame this resentment to cause havoc in the church.

Paul tells Timothy that he is to '*Command* certain men not to teach false doctrines' (1 Tim. 1:3). The same word, 'command', is also used in 1 Timothy 4:11 and 6:17-18. But people do not like being commanded, especially when they are wrong, so the one doing the commanding can expect criticism. Because of this, certain qualities are essential for leaders. The elder must not be violent or quarrelsome but gentle (1 Tim. 3:3). This is necessary because if elders were to react in the same way as they are sometimes treated there would be civil war in the church. Deacons must be men worthy of respect (1 Tim. 3:8). This respect will have been earned over a period of time and Christians will have learnt to trust them and value their opinions. This will be of immense value in defusing difficult situations.

Pastor and elder

The New Testament has much to say about elders though it does not always call them by this name. Sometimes they are also called 'bishops' or 'overseers'. This is clearly seen in Titus 1:5-7, where the words 'elder' and 'overseer' are used to describe the same function. 'Bishop' means the same as 'overseer' and, unlike today, when one bishop has responsibility for several churches, in the New Testament one church had several bishops/overseers/elders. So we read in Acts 20:17 of the elders (plural) of the church at Ephesus.

In 1 Timothy 5:17 Paul seems to suggest that there are two types of elders: those who direct the affairs of the church, and those whose work is preaching and teaching. These are normally known as ruling elders and preaching elders, or more usually in our churches today as elders and pastors. All elders direct the affairs of the church but some have a particular responsibility for preaching. They specialize in this, work hard at it, give time and study to preparation for preaching and as such they are paid by the church (1 Tim. 5:17-18).

The pastor is a teaching elder — his prime responsibility is the ministry of the Word — but all elders share to a degree in this responsibility because all should be able to teach (1 Tim. 3:2). This does not mean that every elder should be able to preach, but because his ministry is spiritual, he must be able to direct and counsel Christians in a personal one-to-one ministry. Therefore in the words of Titus 1:9: 'He must hold firmly to the trustworthy message as it has been taught, so that he can encourage others by sound doctrine and refute those who oppose it.'

Paul has several things to say to Timothy as a pastor and preacher that are applicable to all pastors and preachers. The pastor is a man with a special gift (1 Tim. 4:14). This will include the natural abilities of speech and intelligence, but it is far more than that, as the verse makes clear. He has been given a special gift from God, bestowed upon him by the Holy Spirit and recognized by the church. It is this alone that qualifies him for ministry. The gift must be carefully guarded and not neglected. This is done by the pastor's own spiritual relationship with God and the truths of God: 'Be diligent in these matters; give yourself wholly to them, so that everyone may see your progress. Watch your life and doctrine closely. Persevere in them, because if you do, you will save both yourself and your hearers.' Furthermore, a good minister will preach the truth to the church, even though at times it is not popular (1 Tim. 4:6), and he will not be sidetracked by irrelevancies (1 Tim. 4:7).

The elder is to rule. The function of leadership is to lead and not to wait for a consensus of opinion. But this leadership is not to be domineering: rather it is the leadership of the shepherd whose prime concern is for the well-being of the flock (1 Peter 5:2-3). He leads by the personal example of his life shown in his enthusiasm and diligence for the work of the gospel and for the church (Titus 1:7-8). How should the church behave towards these men?

We should see them as appointed by God (Acts 20:28). As such we should honour them (1 Tim. 5:17) and treat them with respect because of their office. They are not above criticism but the church must be careful as to how it deals with accusations against an elder (1 Tim. 5:19). The reputation of an elder must not be unnecessarily damaged and his work hindered. None the less, if an elder is guilty of sin it is such a serious matter that he must be publicly rebuked (1 Tim. 5:20).

Deacons

The qualifications required for a deacon in 1 Timothy 3 are very similar to those for elders. This is because the difference between the two offices is functional, not one of character. It is not that the elders are more spiritual men than the deacons, but that their gifts and calling are different.

There is little said in this epistle concerning the function of deacons. It is usually believed that the origin of deacons is found in Acts 6, where they were appointed to deal with a serious material problem in the church and thus leave the apostles free to get on with prayer and preaching. Deacons who serve well gain an excellent standing (1 Tim. 3:13). Their reward is the respect and appreciation of the church and this should be given unreservedly and regularly.

6.
The problems of the church

We might be tempted to think that the problems of the Christian church today would be different from those of the church two thousand years ago when Paul was writing to Timothy. But they are basically still the same. Timothy was the pastor of the church at Ephesus and Paul in his epistle to that church said, 'Our struggle is not against flesh and blood, but against the rulers, against the authorities, against the powers of this dark world and against the spiritual forces of evil in the heavenly realms.' Satan was the enemy of the church in Timothy's day and he still opposes God's people in our day.

Satan's ploy is to weaken the church and render it ineffective. Basically he has two methods of doing this: external and internal pressures. In the first century the external pressures were persecution. These were frequent and severe and many believers were killed, but very often the persecution was not effective and, instead of weakening the church, it only strengthened it. Tertullian, writing in the third century, said that the blood of the martyrs became the seed of the church. In other words, the church grew under persecution.

Much more effective are Satan's internal pressures and foremost among them is false doctrine. The church is the pillar and foundation of the truth. False doctrine attacks the truth and is therefore deadly. This is why the New Testament writers give a great deal of space to opposing false teachers and their doctrines: 'But there were also false prophets among the people, just as there will be false teachers among you. They will secretly introduce destructive heresies, even denying the sovereign Lord who bought them — bringing swift destruction on themselves. Many will follow their shameful ways and will bring the way of truth into disrepute' (2 Peter 2:1-2). 'Many deceivers, who do not acknowledge Jesus Christ as coming in the flesh, have gone out into the world. Any such person is the deceiver and the antichrist... If anyone comes to you and does not bring this teaching, do not take him into your house or welcome him. Anyone who welcomes him shares in his wicked work' (2 John 7,10-11). 'Dear friends, although I was very eager to write to you about the salvation we share, I felt I had to write and urge you to contend for the faith that was once for all entrusted to the saints. For certain men whose condemnation was written about long ago have secretly slipped in among you. They are godless men, who change the grace of our God into a licence for immorality and deny Jesus Christ our only Sovereign and Lord' (Jude 3-4).

What is false doctrine?

In answering this we must be careful to maintain the fact that Christians can have genuine differences in their interpretation of Scripture. So if someone does not agree with us on the meaning of a biblical passage, that does not of necessity mean he is a false teacher. False doctrine will do two things: it will rob God of his glory; and it will lead men to hell by teaching a way of salvation other than through Christ alone.

In 1 Timothy Paul tells us two things about false doctrine that are of supreme importance. Firstly, it is satanic — it consists of 'things taught by demons' (4:1); and secondly, it will not conform to the glorious gospel (1:10-11). These two facts are not to be forgotten when dealing with false doctrine. Because it is satanic it is clever. The devil is no fool and the Bible talks of his guile and cunning. For instance, not all false doctrine is obviously unscriptural and many a fine Christian who loves the Lord has been deceived. Mormons or Jehovah's Witnesses may knock at your door, and with an open Bible in their hands, they will quote verses to you. Unless you really know your Bible they could sound very plausible, but what they are doing is quoting verses out of context and giving them a meaning the rest of Scripture would not support. Take, for instance, the Mormon teaching on baptism for dead relatives. On the basis of 1 Corinthians 15:29, they say baptism is essential for salvation. So if people die unbaptized they are lost eternally; however, the living, they believe, may be baptized on behalf of the dead. Whatever 1 Corinthians 15:29 means, it does not teach salvation for the dead by the baptism of the living. This is contrary to the glorious gospel and does not conform to the revealed truth of Scripture.

False doctrine is the most deadly enemy biblical Christianity has to face, so the New Testament writers do not mince words in dealing with it. They do not plead tolerance for false teachers; rather, Paul says, these men are hypocritical liars (1 Tim. 4:2) and are ignorant and conceited (1 Tim. 6:4). We may think this very harsh and consequently may tolerate a poison that will destroy the church, but the New Testament says we are to reject false doctrine as the work of Satan.

False teaching must be opposed

Whatever the reason for false teaching, whether it is propagated by men who 'have wandered away from the truth out of ignorance and arrogance' (1 Tim. 1:6-7), or by men who are hypocritical liars (1 Tim. 4:2), it must be firmly dealt with. Timothy is told that he must command these teachers to stop their false teaching. If this is not successful more severe measures must be taken. They are to be 'handed over to Satan' (1 Tim. 1:20). The best means of opposing false teaching is by a faithful exposition of the truth, so Timothy is told to devote himself to the preaching and teaching of Scripture (1 Tim. 4:13). By doing this he will be a good minister and a means of blessing to the church (1 Tim. 4:6). But some Christians will be deceived by the wrong teachings. How are they to be helped? They are not to be ignored or cut off but patiently wooed. They are the wounded of the battle and every effort must be made to bring them back to full spiritual health.

What if this loving approach fails? In his reference

to Hymenaeus and Alexander (1 Tim. 1:20) Paul re-
minds us that these men were believers who had
shipwrecked their faith. False teaching had taken such
a grip on them that Hymenaeus was teaching that the
resurrection had already taken place. This had to be
dealt with firmly for two reasons: firstly, because false
doctrine can spread like gangrene through the church
and destroy the faith of other believers (2 Tim. 2:17-
18); and, secondly, for the sake of men like Hymenaeus
and Alexander, so that they may be 'taught not to
blaspheme' (1 Tim. 1:20). To this end Paul handed
them over to Satan.

In 1 Corinthians 5 Paul deals with another problem
in the church, namely that of a Christian who was guilty
of sexual immorality. The Corinthian church was commanded to hand the man over to Satan 'so that the sinful
nature may be destroyed and his spirit saved on the day
of the Lord' (v. 5). This is a difficult verse and there
seem to be two possible meanings:

1. It may mean that they are put out of the fellowship of the church, excommunicated (1 Cor.
5:2). This is the interpretation John Calvin took:
'For as Christ reigns in the church, so Satan
reigns out of the church.' So then, Calvin went

on, 'He who is cast out of the church is in a manner delivered over to the power of Satan.'

2. William Hendriksen implies that it means more than excommunication. It may have included also some form of bodily suffering or disease. He writes, 'This extraordinary gift, namely, to commit a person to Satan's power, in order that he might suffer anguish not only in soul but also in body, may strike us as unbelievable, but is it, after all, so strange that added to the charismatic gift of bodily healing was the power to inflict bodily suffering? If we deny the latter, should we not also deny the former?' Hendriksen goes on to stress that the purpose was remedial — not damnation but reclamation being the objective.

Both interpretations emphasize the seriousness of the problem. It is so serious that no church should do it hastily but only in extreme circumstances. It is so serious that if a man really is a Christian he will tremble at the possibility of its happening to him. But the point is that false doctrine is so terrible a disease that no church can tolerate it, and even the most extreme measures must be taken to counteract it.

The doctrinal health of the church is of paramount importance in the New Testament. False teachers may be lovely, kind, charming men but their doctrine is poison. The same problem existed in the Old Testament and the Lord God said it did two things: 'You disheartened the righteous with your lies, when I had brought them no grief, and you encouraged the wicked not to turn from their evil ways and so save their lives' (Ezek. 13:22).

7.
The women of the church

There are two attitudes we can adopt with regard to the teaching in 1 Timothy on the role of women in the church. We can say that Paul was a crusty old bachelor with a bias against women and then ignore all he says on the subject. Or we can say this is part of the inspired Word of God and accept it gladly.

The first viewpoint completely destroys any doctrine of the inspiration and authority of Scripture, and there are few things more serious than that. But also it is untrue that Paul had a bias against women. On the contrary, in Romans 16 he mentions, with obvious joy and great esteem, Phoebe, Priscilla, Mary, Persis and Julia. In Galatians 3:28 he emphasizes that in Christ there is neither male nor female but, as the context there makes clear, he is talking of salvation, not ministry. Can there be a greater regard for women than that manifested in Ephesians 5:25, where men are urged to love their wives just as Christ loved the church, and again in verse 28, where husbands are told to love their wives as they love their own bodies? On the basis of these few scriptures we can dismiss this viewpoint as untrue and arid nonsense.

We are then left with a view that the teaching here on women in the church is part of God's will for his people and therefore we must seek to understand and obey it.

The attitude of women (2:9-10)

These verses refer to women who profess to worship God. When they actually come into the church to worship, extravagance and showiness in dress would be most inappropriate. Their attitude to dress and appearance is not to be governed primarily by fashion or what they can afford but by what is appropriate for women who profess to worship God. It is true that God does not look at the outward appearance but at the heart, but the outward appearance is often a reflection of what is in the heart.

Christian women should not try to show off by wearing flashy or expensive clothes that would cause others to envy them but, says William Hendriksen, 'They do not have to baulk at fashion, unless a particular fashion happens to be immoral or indecent. They must not look decidedly old-fashioned, awkward, or queer. It must ever be borne in mind that a proud heart is sometimes concealed behind a mask of pretended modesty. That too is sin. Extremes must be carefully avoided.' As a Christian woman comes to church to worship God her aim should not be to draw attention to herself by her appearance. After all, the real beauty of a Christian woman is in her character (1 Peter 3:3-4). Of course, the same principle applies equally to men. Our attitude in approaching God must not have any Pharisaic element in it, either in how we look or how we think.

The ministry of women in the church

We are told very clearly what a woman's ministry is not. 1 Timothy 2:12 is very clear: a woman must not exercise a public teaching ministry. This is not referring to women teaching other women or children, but unquestionably it is saying, 'No women preachers in public worship.' The public teacher of God's Word does not only tell others what they need to know, but in his capacity as teacher or preacher he stands before the congregation with authority to rule and govern it by the Word. For a woman to step into this place would be to violate the very Word she is trying to teach. Her efforts to do so would be self-contradictory in God's sight, no matter what the world might say. Paul cannot permit this because God's Word will not permit it (see also 1 Cor. 14:34).

To many people this may seem very old-fashioned at the end of the twentieth century, but this is what the Bible says, and therefore the real issue is not women preachers but the authority of Scripture.

Paul goes on in the following verses to give biblical reasons for his teaching. God made man and woman in such a manner that it is natural for him to lead and for her to follow. She was made to be a help for man and not to be head over him. The terrible story of the Fall in Genesis 3 starts with Eve deciding to lead instead of follow, and of Adam relinquishing his God-given responsibility to lead. Paul says, 'Adam was not the one deceived; it was the woman who was deceived and became a sinner' (1 Tim. 2:14). He does not say this to excuse Adam and blame Eve. In Romans 5 he shows clearly it was the man Adam who was ultimately responsible, but nevertheless Eve disobeyed God's will by leading and therefore trouble was inevitable.

The lesson in 1 Timothy is: do not let the daughters of Eve follow this disastrous example.

Public preaching and teaching are not a woman's ministry. So what is the role of a Christian woman? Part of the answer to this is given in 1 Timothy 2:15: 'But women will be kept safe [or saved] through childbirth, if they continue in faith, love and holiness with propriety.' This does not mean that child-bearing is a way to eternal salvation for women. Salvation is always, for women and men, by grace through faith. Paul is dealing here with Christian women, that is, with women who have already been saved by grace. Real happiness and fulfilment for a Christian woman can only come through obedience to God's will. So instead of hankering after a ministry God has forbidden her to do, she should choose that ministry for which she is naturally equipped by God both physically and spiritually.

The ministry of motherhood is of immense importance and women ought to value it, cherish it and do nothing to undervalue it. Closely associated with this is another ministry of women mentioned in 1 Timothy 5: 'But if a widow has children or grandchildren, these should learn first of all to put their religion into practice by caring for their own family and so repaying their parents and grandparents, for this is pleasing to God.' 'If any woman who is a believer has widows in her family, she should help them' (1 Tim. 5:4,16). These verses are self-explanatory but the important thing is that this is pleasing to God; therefore it should take precedence over everything for a Christian woman. There may be other ministries, such as those of a missionary or a nurse, but they do not supersede what is specifically said to please God. That may not be the way of the world, but it is God's way. Of a mother or housewife the world says she is 'only a housewife', but God says, 'You are a treasure whose worth is far above rubies' (see the last chapter of Proverbs).

The needs of women

In 1 Timothy 5, from verse 3 onwards, the apostle deals with women's needs and the church's responsibilities towards them. The prime responsibility for widows belongs to the family, but those widows with no family are to be helped by the church. They are put on the list (v. 9). This list probably refers to a system of regular financial and material support as seen in Acts 6.

The needs of widows in the first century were obviously more acute than today with all the social and charitable help available, but God has also given the church a firm responsibility to care for its own widows. How this is to be faced up to, each church must decide for itself, but it cannot be avoided. In most churches widows greatly outnumber widowers and many of these old ladies have to face their last days on earth in homes run by unbelievers for unbelievers. Physically they are well looked after, but spiritually there is nothing for them in many of these homes. Can the churches be happy with such a situation? Many churches have faced up to the challenge and established homes for their old folk. It is expensive, but isn't this a modern application of the list?

8.
The money of the church

Paul is concerned about the spiritual health of the church and particularly about God's glory in the church. So, as we have seen, in 1 Timothy he deals with several basic issues, and in the last chapter he brings before us the question of the church's attitude to money. This may appear to some to be a surprising subject to include. But no church can function properly without money. Whether it is paying its ministry, or charitable gifts, or the care of the needy — all of which are dealt with in this epistle — it costs money. And money does not appear mysteriously in the church's bank account by a divine act. God expects his people to supply it out of what he gives them.

So it is not surprising that the New Testament gives a fair amount of space to this basic issue. Whether it is the teaching of Jesus on the widow's mite, or the sections in the Corinthian epistles, the matter is dealt with as a spiritual business of some importance. After the amazing heights and glory of 1 Corinthians 15, with its teaching on resurrection, immediately in the first verse of chapter 16 Paul writes, 'Now about the collection for God's people…' This is not coming down to earth with a bump but all part of the rich revelation of God's will and purpose for his church. In the same way Paul writes in 2 Corinthians 8:7, 'But just as you excel in everything — in faith, in speech, in knowledge, in complete earnestness and in your love for us — see that you also excel in this grace of giving.' The 'grace of giving' is a lovely phrase and the apostle puts it into the context of the grace of God, so that two verses later he says, 'For you know the grace of our Lord Jesus Christ, that though he was rich, yet for your sakes he became poor, so that you through his poverty might become rich.' Writing to Timothy, Paul is concerned about the attitude of Christians towards money and, in particular, two types of Christians: Christians who *are* rich, and Christians who *want to be* rich.

Christians who are rich (6:17-19)

Our first reaction to these verses may be to say that this has nothing to do with me because I am not rich. But rich is a relative term. Compared with Christians in the Third World, most believers in Britain and the USA are very rich. Even compared with Christians in our own country of fifty years ago, we are rich. Many now own their own homes, own a car and telephone and take holidays away from home. For most believers in the first half of the twentieth century these things would only have been a dream.

Material prosperity for the Christian brings with it a great responsibility and also very real dangers. The responsibility is spelt out in verse 18: 'Command them to do good, to be rich in good deeds, and to be generous and willing to share'; and the danger in verse 17: 'Command those who are rich in this present world not to be arrogant nor to put their hope in wealth, which is so uncertain, but to put their hope in God, who richly provides us with everything for our enjoyment.' Note the word 'command' in these verses. Generally speaking, in the world wealth brings with it power and influence. Rich people do not take commands; they give them — but not in the church. In the church, whether a man is rich or poor should have no bearing on his influence or position. The rich and the poor are under the same pastoral care and discipline; so Timothy is told, in his role as pastor, to command the rich as to the correct use of their money.

This will not be easy for any pastor, and he will probably be told to mind his own business. The rich man could say, 'How I spend my money is my business, not the church's.' And to a degree he would be right. But the command here is not one of interference, but of pastoral care for his spiritual well-being. It is to encourage the rich to put their hope in God and not money, and thus to take hold of the life that is truly abundant.

How would you react if your pastor told you that your use of money was all wrong? Would you be angry and move to another church? Or would you acknowledge that he was performing a God-given duty and give serious thought to whether or not he might be right. We hear of certain charismatic groups where all the members' property and money has to be under the control of the church. We may believe that to be wrong, and rightly so, but how much better is our own attitude to our money and possessions? Do we use what we have to do good? Are we generous and willing to share? Is the spirit of Acts 4:34-35 true of churches today?

Material prosperity can easily lead to materialism (1 Tim. 6:17). It need not do this and the remedy is also found in verse 17. There is nothing wrong in having possessions: what is wrong is to *trust in* them and not in God. It is wrong to allow what we have to make us arrogant and think we are better than other believers. To use what we have for the glory of God and the well-being of others is to lay up treasures in heaven.

Christians who want to be rich (6:9-10)

If riches can be a problem for some Christians, for others an even greater problem is a longing to be rich. It fosters a spirit of envy, jealousy and dissatisfaction. The person who craves riches generally also yearns for honour, popularity and power. He may cloak all this by covering his cravings with a veneer of good motives. He may say that if he was rich he could do so much good, but his real motive is greed and the end will be spiritually disastrous.

It is not money, but the *love* of money that is a root of all kinds of evil. It is not the only root of evil, but it is certainly one of the major ones. The love of money, particularly money you do not have, can even cause a believer to wander from the faith. Consider some of the problems a love of money develops in a Christian.

1. It will cause him to be unfaithful in his stewardship. Such a Christian will never tithe and can always justify to himself poor giving to the Lord's work.

2. It will cause him to be unsympathetic to others in need. He will accuse the needy of being lazy and scroungers, and thus refuse to help them.

3. He could become dishonest in his giving like Ananias and Sapphira. He will speak volumes publicly of how Christians ought to give but not do it himself.

It is through attitudes like this that the love of money causes a believer to wander from the faith.

Correct attitudes (6:6-8)

Contentment is the fruit of godliness. It is the product of an inner spiritual strength which provides riches far beyond those the world can imagine. To know and live the truth, 'for we brought nothing into the world, and we can take nothing out of it', is to fix your eyes on treasures in heaven.

To be rich is not wrong for a Christian, but to misuse those riches is. To crave for riches has to be wrong for anyone, but for the Christian it is spiritually deadly. A healthy biblical attitude to money by all believers would mean that the church would never have to cut back its work because of financial reasons. The church would not then ask whether it could afford to start or continue a particular work, but whether it could afford *not* to do so, if that is the direction in which God is leading them.

Conclusion

The devil hates the church because he hates Christ, the Head of the church. It is not surprising, therefore, that he is always seeking to attack the church that Christ loves so much. In the New Testament we can see how this satanic opposition manifests itself.

In its infancy the church had to face bitter persecution from both the state and the religious authorities. This has continued right up to the present time in many countries, but it always fails to destroy Christ's church. In fact it often has the opposite effect. It was said in the early church that the blood of the martyrs became the seed of the church. In other words, persecution strengthened rather than weakened the people of God. But Satan has more than one string to his bow and often his most effective weapon against the church is the lack of Christlikeness in the Christians who make up the membership. He will use our worldliness, shallowness, lack of vision and petty-mindedness to cause havoc in the fellowship. Bitter words and selfish attitudes cause more damage in a church than almost anything else. Therefore Paul's desire that we know how to conduct ourselves in God's household is of prime importance.

The only God-honouring way to behave in church is the way of love as described in 1 Corinthians 13: 'Love is patient, love is kind. It does not envy, it does not boast, it is not proud. It is not rude, it is not self-seeking, it is not easily angered, it keeps no record of wrongs.' Before you start applying these verses to other members of your church, apply them to yourself. Are you envious of other Christians' spiritual gifts? Are you easily upset? Do you keep a record of wrongs, so that there are some believers that you sit with at the communion table but ever hardly talk to? There is an old jingle that we ought to remind ourselves of fairly frequently:

If every member was just like me,
What kind of church would my church be?

Would it be a more prayerful church? Would it be more concerned for the lost and more pleasing to God? To expect your church to be any more spiritual than you are is hypocritical. The church is made up of individuals just like you and me. There are some Christians who are very easy to get on with. Others are more difficult, but we are all members of the household of God, so be patient. Remember that some believers probably find it difficult to get on with you, so be tolerant. Do not let the devil use you to damage the church for which Christ died.

We need to learn how to behave in church and a study of 1 Timothy can help us because basically it means that we learn how to think biblically. To think biblically means that the teaching of Scripture formulates our thinking. Paul put it like this in Philippians 2:5: 'Your attitude should be the same as that of Christ Jesus.' He then goes on to mention later in the same epistle two women in the church at Philippi who were not living like this: 'I plead with Euodia and I plead with Syntyche to agree with each other in the Lord' (Phil. 4:2). We do not know what the problem was between these two women, but clearly it was disturbing Paul and causing trouble in the church. Whatever the particular disagreement, the real problem was that Euodia and Syntyche were not displaying a Christlike attitude. The mind of Christ was humble and lowly, and therefore what these women needed was humility and a willingness for self-sacrifice. But as James Montgomery Boice says in his commentary on Philippians, 'This will never occur apart from a personal and intimate walk with God, for in ourselves we do not like humility. And we cannot achieve it without him. If you are far from the Lord, then frictions will inevitably spring up between yourself and other Christians. The things they say will irk you. The things they do will get under your skin and fester. If this is not to happen, then you must maintain a close and personal fellowship with the Lord. You see, Paul wanted his admonition to the women at Philippi to come down to the personal level. For he knew, as we all should know, that the effectiveness of the Christian warfare depends upon the conduct of the individual Christian soldier.'

How should we behave in church? In a way that pleases Christ; in a way that reflects the mind and attitude of Christ; in a way that encourages our fellow Christians and causes unbelievers to say, 'Behold how these Christians love one another!' It is not easy and it is only possible as we each maintain a close and personal fellowship with the Lord.

For further reading

Peter Jeffery, *Walk worthy,* Evangelical Press of Wales
Clifford Pond, *Only servants,* Grace Publications
Warren Wiersbe, *Be faithful*, Scripture Press
Daniel Wray, *The importance of the local church,*
    Banner of Truth Trust
Daniel Wray, *Biblical church discipline*, Banner of
    Truth

**Other titles
by
Peter Jeffery**

Sickness and Death in the Christian Family

Peter Jeffery

ISBN 0 85234 308 6
Paperback, 112 pages

Starting from the biblical case study of Mary, Martha and Lazarus, the reader is shown how to find help and encouragement in God in times of great personal stress.

It has short, straightforward chapters, and the author draws on his own personal experience and that of great men of God.

The Young Spurgeon

Peter Jeffery

ISBN 0 85234 239 4
Large paperback,
112 pages

Peter Jeffery tells the story of Spurgeon's early years, often in his own words, beginning in his childhood in his grandfather's home, through the thrilling account of his conversion one snowy January morning and his first experience as a preacher, when he was still in his teens, and concluding with a brief overall view of his later life and ministry.

Great God of Wonders
The attributes of God

Peter Jeffery

ISBN 0 85234 302 7
Paperback, 96 pages

This book is written to help those beginning the Christian faith to see something of what God has revealed in Scripture about himself. The atttributes of God do not belong to the realm of theory; they are not mere doctrines that have no bearing upon the Christian's daily living. Rather they are most practical and enriching.